HOW LATE DESIRE LOOKS

HOW LATE DESIRE LOOKS

KATRINA ROBERTS

GIBBS·SMITH
P
PUBLISHER

SALT·LAKE CITY

First Edition

00 99 98 97 5 4 3 2 1

This is s Peregrine Smith Book, published by
Gibbs Smith, Publisher
P.O. Box 667
Layton, UT 84041

Designed by Kathleen Timmerman
Edited by Gail Yngve

Cover art, *St Genevieve Watching over Paris,* by Pierre Puvius de Chavannes

Library of Congress Cataloging-in-Publication Data

Roberts, Katrina.
   How late desire looks / by Katrina Roberts. — 1st ed.
   p. cm.
   ISBN 0-87905-815-3
   I. Title.
PS3568.023975H69   1997
811' .54—dc21
                                         97-740
                                          CIP

Previous winners of the Peregrine Smith Poetry Competition include: *Sequences,*
by Leslie Norris; *Stopping by Home,* by David Huddle; *Daylight Saving,* by Stephen Bauer;
The Ripening Light, by Lucile Adler; *Chimera,* by Carol Frost; *Speaking in Tongues,* by
Maurya Simon; *The Rebel's Silhouette,* by Faiz Ahmed Faiz (translated by Agha Shadid Ali);
The Arrangement of Space, by Martha Collins; *The Nature of Yearning,* by David Huddle;
After Estrangement, by Molly Bendall; *Geocentric,* by Pattiann Rogers; *1-800-HOT-RIBS,*
by Catherine Bowman; *Buying Breakfast for My Kamikaze Pilot,* by Norman Stock;
The Uses of Passion, by Angie Estes; and *Perfect Hell,* by H. L. Hix.

Judging for the competition is done by Christopher Merrill.

for J. F. R. & H. A. R.
& for you,
my secret love

ACKNOWLEDGMENTS

Grateful acknowledgment to the editors of the following journals in which these poems first appeared: *The Antioch Review:* "For Your Departure"; *Boston Book Review:* "Harm's Way," "The Cup"; *Harvard Magazine:* "How Late Desire Looks," "*Always, the Space Between*"; *The Journal:* "About Refusal"; *The North Atlantic Review:* "Granted"; *Painted Bride Quarterly:* "The Ruffled Edge," "Sestina About Reciprocity"; *The Southern Poetry Review: "Vendange."*

"How Late Desire Looks" and "*Always, the Space Between*" were nominated for inclusion in *Pushcart Prize XX: Best of the Small Presses,* and the former appears in *Best American Poetry 1995;* guest editor: Richard Howard. "The Pill" appears in the anthology *Life on the Line;* Negative Capability Press, 1992. "Sestina About Reciprocity" received the 1994 *Painted Bride Quarterly Prize.*

My appreciation, as well, to The MacDowell Colony, the St. Botolph Foundation, and The Massachusetts Cultural Council, for their generous support.

Gratitude to my many teachers and friends, and thanks to Monique Mégy and Mouse. Love always to AJ Dorvillier, and for enduring belief in my work, thanks especially to Jack Marshall, Dorothy Burr, and Paul Lisicky.

CONTENTS

I

II

III

IV

Even if it is quickly cut in two, immediately its inside becomes a wall and there occurs the lightning-swift transformation of a mystery into a skin...

—ZBIGNIEW HERBERT

She followed slowly, taking a long time as though there were some obstacle in the way; and yet: as though, once it was overcome, she would be beyond all walking, and would fly.

—RAINER MARIA RILKE

A snake was never called by its name at night, because it would hear. It was called a string. And so on this particular night as the crier's voice was gradually swallowed up in the distance, silence returned to the world, a vibrant silence made more intense by the universal trill of a million million forest insects.

—CHINUA ACHEBE

I

HOW LATE DESIRE LOOKS

To begin with something not already caught
In the current of another's life, an indifferent
Hand of transparent wind playing first
With the sleeve at your damp wrist, then
Pressing strands of hair sideways against my
Mouth, the beautiful coming, like a gift
Of the rare Indigo Bunting, body turquoise
At your feeder in the slanting light, soft
Particles of air, silting through high aspens
To settle around us like hope itself. I could

Watch you carry a clear glass jar of water
Walking nowhere in particular, at least
Forever—back and forth across your yard
Where five orange poppies, like saucers
Tilt together on slender necks, and scents
Of globe basil, nicotiana and lilies intermix
Because you've cultivated this rocky, sloping
Piece of wilderness into a place to live—
Just for the way what looks in your eyes
Like thirst, holds me contained one minute

Longer than intended, since I'm a neighbor
Merely returning a borrowed bicycle or book
And even now we hear your wife's car grind
Into the drive, arriving, and the startled
Bunting, which is actually black but for a
Complex pattern of diffraction through its
Structure of feathers, suddenly takes off
So that what remains are a few Chickadees,
The most common Yellowthroat, taunting:
Which-is-it, Which-is-it, Which-is-it
And the Grosbeak with its rose-breasted blush.

TERMINOLOGY
—for Kevin

Just a question of nomenclature, this system
    we have for living, especially when we learn
        it's temporary. *Here, now,* and after, *where?*

You say the word, and I try entering with
    you, but through a revolving door I spit
        back out the other side of, while you, *you*

keep spinning, caught between the clear, clean
    sandwiched glass. *There* the foyer, *there*
        the stretching corridors, all

shortening before our eyes ... Or, *no, not really:*
    in fact, you've never looked better—no
        longer smoking, drinking. And here

I envision a station, Grand Central, *hotel de ville,*
    some large portico with soot-blackened cherubs, stone
        garlands serpentine and draped—their permanence

small comfort to what's transient within the walls
    of this magnificent jouncing space where souls wait,
        resting on the edge of seats, then sinking down,

later lifting a creased and glowing cheek from folds of wadded coats.
    Rumpled minds and hair, wings tucked neatly inside
        sweaters (often feverish but cold), mufflers flung

aside, layers looped across legs and slipping ... Flying
    buttresses ... Angles of light my mum calls angels, streaming
        through high arched windows, hazed and

never opened. Two pigeons flap to roost, the iridescent
    noose of jeweled heather, jade gleaming around plump
        necks ... *That terminal* or *this:* the place

you come to go away, where others arrive for *others* almost daily,
    but you stand resolute on platform five, off on your own, tending
        to your lone departure. *Where*

will you be going? Something we all know happens, but something
    that makes a word become a sentence that binds, *terminal—*
        intensifies, clarifies as time has defined your cheekbones.

Your eyes grow big, their blue brindled by candle glint;
    about you there is defiance; say it, *terminal,* is it relief
        I hear ... I'm too young? you *tell* me,

and I feel fear bristling: small cat
    arching its back, spiked fur, sun-drenched
        cement: how far down the tunnel can we see?

When we meet, embrace, all's fine. Then some line drawn between illuminated
    and dark sides of a disk moon that is *this* white saucer, this bright *now,*
        that dim future, half the plate hidden beneath a puddle

of German chocolate sauce, the other, soft curds of tiramisu: clods
    of earth, and clouds. I take my fork to marble both, nibble
        the mint garnish. I like to think of this in other terms:

the ornamental carving high above our heads, stone medallion bathed
    in afternoon sun for homebound honking traffic; or a kind of juncture
        in sound: a pause *between,* a rising, a falling, a sustained note

after an utterance. *Um,* I say later, lingering, dallying the spoon
    in leftover creme: a necessary silence, honoring your fear or
        reverence ... If we are armed

forces, you're enjoying a kind of
    terminal leave—immediately before discharge,
        ... accumulated unused time; how

will you use it now, knowing knowledge
    will never change? *Cure?* Would that there were
        already; you're thirty, vital, high in life's swing

and yet ... I picture Terminus, ghosting your mother's shoulder (*she*—
    diagnosed last year with cancer, now riddled. You watched her pull
        her hair in wads and told her; now you share. *Who first?*)

—*Terminus,* that Roman deity, presiding over landmarks and boundaries.
    What will your mother's stone read? Years you were Trimalchio, toga-ed
        friend of Bacchus; orgies and girls, boys and booze and bed.

These daily implements: shaker for salt, fork, glass of gin, all
    becoming stone markers, cairns delineating what life once
        was. *Terminus ad quo* and *terminus ad quem*—origins

and ends. And this gorgeous body I want to hold still,
    this body I want to still in its steady falling ... but already
        the terminal velocity, the frictional resistance of air ...

What lets you go, slide ... air, the enveloping medium
    equal to the force of gravity ... and no feathers to catch
        the downdraft. Arms, extremities flailing or graceful ...

terminal feather, terminal leaf, new growth at the end, last
    stop, place to get off, find your next ride, change directions, either end
        of the line for plane, bus, train, facilities included so use 'em

while you can ... This body before me, this mind. What connects us
    to the current that is *being alive?* Mind, *spinning.* Body,
        benison, *spinning,* and prison ...

and we, third termers—done nothing wrong but
    succumb to life, which is desire, which is love, which
        is contact with others. What is terminable,

this contract with whom? T-cells down by 400.
    A sinking, but with style. I picture the terrapin, vast
        diamondback turtle, *here,* and *now*

gone beneath so many tons and green gallons. We share
    the leftover sauce, and you smile. *You've never looked*
        better. You look at me; I could die.

ROSES UNDER THE TREES

Some things I hide in my heart only to find offered freely
By others with upturned palms.
What is it about me?

Yesterday I walked through the orchard.
The air was heavy with an oily scent of citrus
And every bough bent down, under its yellow weight.
Such bounty and thick fragrance
I wanted to cry out loud.

I'm not sorry, exactly. I could go back there
Though many of the salmon petals would have let go by now
In the night's rain. Would I learn from them?
Under the trees I could lie and breathe deeply.
I could see the thousand colors which ask nothing of me
As nothing more than shapes of color.
I could give myself to them.
I could comb the green grasses with my opened fingers.

What there would be of sky would be lilac and warm
Or grey, like my eyes. Though mostly
The leaves would obscure it as my heart sometimes hides
What is most dear to me. At least now I know

To look in every drop which clings
To each blade and thorny stem or bitter lemon
To see reflected there entire worlds of possibility.
Wisps of cloud caught in outstretched branches, globes
Of ripened fruit. Blown roses.

And all composing an easy pattern I must learn to open into.

THINGS THAT LAST ONLY A DAY,
THINGS THAT LAST LONGER

The first day that I couldn't breathe
I sat in a wicker chair working my lungs.
I thought that someone would come,
I kept thinking someone would have to come for me.
Nobody came.
Breathing is something
I usually do alone, even among others. Nobody kept coming.
Breathing is something I usually do.

I felt I had become somebody else
watching myself. As if on film. I felt like someone
who couldn't breathe. Not me.
I distinctly remember my hands, each of them, and my two knees.

The day that I couldn't breathe I stayed all day
in a chair with woven ribs, waiting. In the corner
of a small glass room, I sat facing south and slightly
east, the direction the chair faced when I found it.
I lit one match before sitting. I struck it and sniffed shallowly
the way a cat would. I cupped my hand around empty air
like an apple. I kept it from sputtering out.
I watched the day's headlines catch. I watched
the day burn out, another catch, yesterday. Nothing mattered
but breathing and heat.
I watched the stove eat all the air. Nobody came.

I sat with each of my elbows
bent by each of my sides. I could have been
carrying a tray of air in front of my chest, my heart, my lungs.
I watched the flames' hundreds of tongues. *Where are you?*
I wished to cry out.
I kept thinking about my lungs, picturing.
With my elbows bent I waited for some indication. I tell you,
I waited. I watched the star
jasmine, tendrils shooting and twining, the creeping
ivy with its heart-shaped leaves and
the wandering Jew. Starting in morning
I watched two red blossoms, like lungs I thought,
begin to unfold, unfurl slowly in the sun.

They could have been tiny lungs, I thought as I waited
and watched. I thought about waiting. I thought
about breathing. I waited to breathe. I tried
to wait patiently. It is hard
to wait patiently when what you are

8

is waiting to breathe. Imagine it, not breathing.
I thought about not breathing. Not breathing is
not the same as holding your breath. I thought about lungs, all
of them, each one not working. I thought about thinking
about not breathing, and that made it worse.
I think I waited patiently, considering.
All that time I was waiting, I would have liked to have been
holding your hand. All the time I was thinking
about trying, and trying
to breathe, I would have been happy to hold your hand.
I kept wondering whether there would be another
day. Or somebody coming.
There is always another day, I thought
but usually I can breathe.

I didn't yet know you, the day of my trying
to breathe. If I had known you, if I had been able to hold in my mind
like air in my lungs the thought of you coming, the breathing
might have known on its own what to do.

That was the first day I couldn't breathe.
That was the worst.
There have been others since. The panic starts
like a small black thing. A seed, the opposite of flame—
though it spreads that way in the chest
as if eating. But more like a cold spill or seeping
of something dark, a liquid, a shadow
across the chest. A pressing, a pressure. Once a lover
squeezed me so hard in his arms I stopped breathing. The day
that I couldn't breathe, I remembered his fingers
squeezing. His hands were small like a woman's.

I watched each red petal open like fingers.
I watched as I waited to breathe.
All day I looked at the sticky stamens,
yellow with pollen. I looked at the pistil.
I tried to unfold, tried to let my lungs
fill with air. I was alone and I couldn't breathe.

I'm telling you this because at the end of the day
both blossoms dropped. Like hands
they let go and fell to the tile as I watched.
They gave back an expanded air, and at last
I started to breathe. *In, out.* It helps
to know that there are things that last only a day, things
that last longer. Of course
I could never forget any of this. I didn't yet know you. I'm sorry.

the scales of pale light   and the thread of breath exhaled
perhaps the (coming unstitched)   last wish from the
dying heart, the light   dying, its subtle
ritual intinction—a slipping   of mind into brightness
seeped upward,   always the space (not) left
between the wisdom of something   instinctual and solid
for example, the sudden   looming of shoulders
and then, the darker shadow   of (something!) just behind
the shoulders—makes a question   out of the weight
of light just above them   and everything else.
The gradation is only visible   (and the long running-stitch
of light meaning Door   and the Go on—touch it, sip
it, put your lips   against this last (hands) glass—there
where the   lips touch glass touch water touch air) there
along the seams, when   a dazzling innocence streams
milky blue   from the eye not extinguished and
the mind surmounting through space   (
what is the weight of the space, again   again?)
has not yet   let go and still rushes its how many
hands in to ease the   ideas (fish) darting (copper coins
for the eyes)   streaming like fracting/
refracting light slicing the dying   room in two pieces,
each flooded   (flooding the ears eyes nose mouth please
stay please where are you   now and) always, with sound.

SESTINA ABOUT RESTRAINT

Possibility lies at our feet
        like a smooth cream envelope.
It sleeps, still sealed, in a lacquered tray
        on the mahogany mailstand with its blue
glass knobs. We think of an obedient pet,
        waiting patiently by the crackling fire
to be walked. Tongues of flame rose-tint
        our upturned faces. We discuss when
it could have been sent, from where, and how
        it has found us here, at a moment just
as we were deciding all its remnants had
        been borne off by a swirling, dust-filled wind.

We speak in metaphors, our intentions
        the hidden spools we let language wind
around. You are wise and know many things.
        Your stories envelop
me with their resonances, the seduction of hearing
        in your voice not just
facts but hints. A stamp, the high-up window
        in our whitewashed wall, a blue
gulf swimmed through by stars, validates us
        with some weight of worldly things. When
we close one eye at a time, the image shifts
        away from us, each single bright fire

a lightning bug zipping across the field. We
        laugh. How long ago these fires
burned out, and yet still they seem to shine
        for us! We tell lies, shifting like wind
from north to east to fill, deflate, then fill
        again our spinnakers. Of course, when
we open it, there is no guarantee that what
        will spill from the well-traveled envelope
will not disappoint us. Ashes, orange peels, dust,
        bits of dried yellow flowers and blue
feathers, trinkets perhaps intended for someone
        else, after all, someone just

like us in many ways, but not actually us. Our
        world is a just world for some, unjust
for others. The dog wants desperately to go out,
        but also lives to please. Fire
first warms but then destroys, consumes at times
        like love just what's most loved. Blue

flames lick, an emerald serpent's forked tongue;
five black crows ride the wind
above an old red barn. Our names scrawled in ink
across the snowy field of envelope
resemble a winter wind fence: stoic, elegant,
broken, dipping, running away just when

all we want to do is hold each other, contain
each other in this love envelope, when
all we want to do is hear each other, spill into
each other's ears and bodies just
as a river does, parting. It spreads, crashes
into an onrushing sea, the crisp envelopes
of its waves like legs parting to let seconds
then thirds break through. I'm on fire.
Two red fish swim in a clear glass bowl. They
have never felt the caress of a wind
but there must be something similar in their world.
I approach the river. The bluish-

black surface ripples; the pebbles gleam beneath
like teeth. The tongue of the blue
current carries us downstream quickly. Step
into it twice, that river, the minute when
you feel it is most unlikely you'll do anything
important again. When you feel winded,
slow your pace but carry on. We cannot afford
to stop. Each experience is just
exactly what we need. The envelope is fat, heavy,
foreign but familiar. The fire
suddenly sends blue sparks across the carpet,
confetti tossed from the envelope

of our hearth like hope or at least its possibility.
The dog, Azul, wakes and barks just
when the grandfather clock strikes an hour. We must
step into the same waters and fires far
more often than twice. Where will this all wind up?
To know, we must climb into the open envelope.

AT THE LARK

Nothing here is as old as that
which we so desire.
To the uninitiated, how closely
any new establishment
might resemble every potential other
in an attractiveness particular
to all winged things especially.

Often on this highway
lights appear to veer directly toward us.
Of course it matters.

More and more frequently
I come to realize how we are willing
to give a little, bend north
when the melt, in fact, pools south
to rest in a place ringed entirely
by palms—just because

we want to believe
we have some say in at least a minute part
of this throaty singing.

That we ask for fish broiled, so far
from any sea. No wonder
we feel we are being
difficult! Why, everyone else
is able to enjoy standard cuts of rare
beef, in some starlit lounge, there—

just beyond our willing reach.
It's the tonal approach
we must practice. Though,

we feel quite skilled
at the perfunctory *"all set, thanks"*
and such. So easy
to whisper it really, and yet . . .
Everything always begins
to shimmer around the edges. How
we watch. And we wait. How we listen.

THE PIN

Let it not be said that the pin is a small thing, for it is not. Already it has made you stop to listen.

On a cold night it grows—growing even smaller than one might imagine, but somehow it sharpens concurrently, like an eyebeam from the woods. Turn your headlights upon it there, under the trees: the sight of its diminutiveness pierces your heart. In this moment, a thousand misplaced stories will burst into flame, and the smoke from that blaze will cling to your woolen clothing. You see, there are certain scents one cannot shake. For example, apprehension. All right. Now, drive on.

So, you believe that one either lives or does not live; I would like to propose the pin— as a juncture between two extremes. Look, our blood mixes.

*

Let me begin again. Where did you find it, this pin?

What have I done? I have ruined something immense with one tiny slip in the wrong direction. Something hangs deflated between us. Our repair cannot be seamless, if there is to be one—for thread will not follow the needle without an eye. But, this clean little knot of metal will keep us fastened together loosely, at least until we've reached some sort of safety.

*

So, if she said, "*The Architect of Time will arrive for luncheon at twelve,*" would you bat an eyelash? Would you worry that the afternoon might slip into evening, that dirty dishes would go unnoticed, despite the sweeping hands of the clock? Prick your finger; this is not a Dali painting.

Cousin to many, this splinter of steel. Such display of frippery overwhelms. And those plainer relatives become so very important, in moments of necessity.

Incidentally, the debate as to how frequently they ought to be in contact, has continued for years. It has been set to music. It has a life of its own.

The question is really—what kind of juncture will suffice? Should we dress in silk and plumage? Will the choice trinket pinned to her breast be that one fashioned from seed pearls, amethyst, and rubies?

*

I should begin at the front end and tell you the whole story, but the idea is fatiguing. Let me just say that the fascination has been a long one, and those early memories settle into a landscape resembling that where I was first taken to live. I do remember an older brother saying *"hush hush, baby"* all the while pricking me. This initial juxtaposition of pleasure and excruciation is one that I have sought to recreate ever since. Squares of white cotton are easy; it's more difficult to locate someone willing to inflict pain. That is, not only willing, but eager.

So, you think I am unwell? At least I know I am living!

*

Sometimes it happens that she finds it with the soft part of her foot. Other times she sees it glint below the armoire, and then she bends over at the waist to retrieve it.

There is an incendiary quality to her words, her skin, her unmediated movement; to her limbs and hair; to her clothing, wishes, her embraces. If it drops again . . . Precaution would be to weave it through a bit of bright fabric and place it high up on an unreachable shelf.

That, or let it exist where it has fallen.

There are always others, glinting within the cellophane package. But they all go through her in such different ways. And despite care, each leaves a tiny hole somewhere. How often has she stood out in the eye of a squall, precisely waiting to feel the needling sensation against her cheeks? How often has she gone out into it again? And what does she prefer—the pin or the fact of its being there and now not there any more?

Glinting like train tracks through fields of cotton—pins she jabs in to indicate the line for stitching. Sun punctures the panes. Invisible seams seem to be preferable, but she cuts the process of the hem line short (or, rather—draws it longer) by letting the garment slip from her hands into the basket, and she goes outdoors. From the garden, inside bay windows, she can see fine metal stitches. They speak to her through clenched teeth. *I can't,* she answers.

*

If you remain extremely quiet, on occasion you may hear the voice of the pin. And if you guessed, then you are correct—it is particularly high in pitch, perhaps owing to its minuteness and the compression of energy required of it to contain itself in such a small body of light. If you were to drop it into the sea, or a glass of water for that matter, with the intention of losing it, well of course then you would not hear its deafening cry; however,

if you let it go in order to keep a part of it (despite its smallness) always close to you, then its voice would overwhelm you (and you would probably dive in after it. In fact, many men have been lost in just this manner.)

*

15

For a moment, let us imagine the exquisite construction of such a body. Produced en masse and yet... How alone each feels. And in joining others, do they feel diminished? That is difficult to surmise, for the marriage of two may resemble the conjunction of another two, or in absolutely no way whatsoever. And, depending upon the restriction stemming from the point of fixture, the arms will pivot in tight, frictional increments or swing freely 360 degrees—always fastened at the heart but not affixed at all points.

*

Anyway, it is not enough to be entranced by the idea of it; you must want to wholeheartedly embrace it.

Sometimes it is merely useful.

Sometimes it is not at all for anything save to decorate the ear through which it's stuck. I don't know where he got it, the idea of it even, this dark, young leather-clad character. It is the spaces, the holes in random places, the space between front teeth. The intricate attractiveness of his torn lobe. The awkwardness attracts me. Young, yes, and innocent? But he would give it to me if I asked.

No. I don't mean that. It is not so much the object of the pin, but his intention for it? The diversity of interpretation staggers us all. What then? Why don't we just agree on letting it rest between us? If angels dance above your head while down below...

let go.

Sometimes it is more than useful.

For example, I remember her sitting in an alcove of sorts awaiting his return and then, mouth full of pins (a handy place to store them while one mends), she couldn't kiss him.

*

(That's the thing of course, the relativity of it. Seen from the sky it lies like a thin body of water. If you were fortunate enough to take a journey down it, floating in a pod-canoe, you would realize that though the solidity of its walls gives way to air rapidly (the pin's length being not particularly long) the direction either end points leads toward a veritable eternity. We created it, with block and die. Among siblings it will remain, cool, despite internal boiling, emitting a clean scent not unlike that of carbonated water. Its sharp breathing, of course, would be imperceptible, save for the infinitesimal bubbles rising—like translucent and ancient trees—toward light. Let me, then, suggest the pin, with its disposition for departure, as a point of quiet origin.

16

II

VENDANGE

As soon as she woke she knew
already he had gone out
to tinker with boats or fish
on the jetty with the other men
she thought probably
I am furthest from his thoughts

Below in the kitchen the cook
deciding for dinner upon fresh
trout & green beans with almonds
sent a small boy clattering
down the back stairs to the cellar
Smelling of mints the composer
who lived over the market next door
poured himself a second
coffee & again sat down to play

Parting the white lace curtains &
dressing she then descended to find
a place set for one in the café
under the trees whose yellowing
leaves the rain had mostly
brought down & she wrapped
her scarf closer

She knew it was over & the far-off
boom of cannons
which sent thick vast clouds
of birds from the glistening vines
& the grapes not yet harvested
startled not only her but
the swan she had seen
the day before with a fishhook

caught in his head who
suddenly began to beat & beat
his great white wings
against the surface at the lake's
closest rim thereby rising &
hovering for a moment
like forgiveness itself she
thought almost angelic
above the dark & pleating water

THE HEAT WHEN SHE RETURNS

When she returns, she is met not with festivity but by death. Crepe paper garlands
    stick limply against the fluted
pillars, their blackness so very piteous, the way it calls attention to itself in the midst
    of the tiresome, pale, midday
air. Snaking its way out of town, the long line of cars is endless in the stifling heat.
    They move carefully now in lines
like insects, but slowly, oh so slowly and cautiously up the hill toward the sky which
    hangs like some thick grey fog
or a disease no one talks about—and if they do, it's in yellow tones and they avoid
    the important part with a big
swerve, as though moving around the back hooves of the one sad ox in the barn.
    She fears they may fill up

the house, finally, swell it, rushing into all possible spaces like heat, or tears. She
    pictures water rising—briny
warm water sloshing first around all their stockinged ankles, then swelling, swelling
    and soon . . . his bed will lift, swirl
in one eddying turn and drift up and off. She imagines squares of bright light. A
    white cotton flag. But
then, unintentionally jostling her elbow, one of the thick-wristed men mops his neck
    with a handkerchief, and back
she comes. Each hand carries wilting lettuce or a cucumber salad, sliced pink ham
    sweating saltily. They are
not hungry, any of them. They are nauseated, but, they leave these mounds of food.
    The cat stretched mid-

doorway cocks an ear, quivers a bit as the ham passes and looks for some small breeze.
    The coo hoo, *hoo hoo hoo*
of the turtledove makes her think of soft waves somewhere else. Coming back to such
    great heat and a small town
and the death of the king's good son, innocent lamb meandering but with a purpose on
    some sleepy southwestern street,
gorged like a piece of meat pierced, skewered through—impaled on a post like a leaf
    on a stick, makes her weary.
Like bullfights, she thinks, pointless, but maybe not. Where she's coming back from,
    the glittering water laps deceptively
easily, the violent sun strokes the blood-smeared cobbles, and the clattering of vain
    voices stirs the air.

It thrills her. But here, bearing down upon them, stifling them like wet silk, the heat
    makes the breathing in, and the breathing
out difficult for all of them, except for him—patched together for his family to see
    and sealed in the long
cool mintlike lozenge, encased in the conditioned room, cool air seeming to breathe
    even from it. His young
wife, her age, and all the people of the town come, and the room fills and the heat
    swells, and she thinks of him

in the cool box locked against the heavy sky, the sick grey day and the weeping,
   wilting, waiting of everyone
for the thunderhead to break through with some relief—as though his death needed
   this senseless August heat

—a constant reminder that ceaseless evil exists, slapping the air. She wonders
   about his lamblike innocence (!),
having read something once about the talons of sin. *My good son,* sobs the king.
   It is unusual to see him cry.
This disturbs the people perhaps more than the death, this shaking of the man who is
   the father. The endless line of cars,
like the one that killed him, moves carefully now still. They come as though drawn
   to the light, fatigued yet
frantically beating their useless wings against some shell of gloom which cloaks the
   house. They come as though
wishing to break through the heat. Coming back to such great heat, she longingly
   hears the Morse code of

one woodpecker tapping from the cool forest, one turtledove softly bemoaning this
   day from the shade, and
she would like to go there now. The crickets are incessant like the wheels of the cars.
   Oh these well-wishers, she thinks,
as in some Tchaikovsky piece and the innocent boy who escaped all the heat—
   heat of the cauldron and fire
in the woods, escaped everything except the crazy yellow eyes, or escaped everything
   because of them ... eyes flickering
like lights, zagging toward him, his army job and slim wife, the car, like a crazed
   animal in the early morning dark
leapt toward him, and in an instant: an impaled letter on a wrought-iron fence.
   She thinks of a letter written

to her once in spindly dark ink, which proclaimed *to like is a lie with an absent* k
   present. Like anything horrifying and
sudden bearing down upon her, pushing and breaking sharp wetly through, it
   makes her cry a bit now also.
This momentary pain which he probably didn't even have time to contemplate, as he
   walked wiping the toast
crumbs from his chin, his eyes still bleary, when Boom! it pierced him messily.
   She curls the hem of her skirt
around one finger, a sleeve slightly sodden, and realizes that this feast is her welcome
   back. She envies his easy
departure. Perhaps the sudden absence of all was a release for him too, she thinks.
   For her it is often—

after the unbearable heat, the pushing, stifling body heavy upon her—finally a relief
   when she feels that stab of
wonderful pain, and the other rolls off. Then she breathes in, watching her lung cage
   rise skyward toward a
place where the ceiling ought to hang, and she swells toward stars glittering like teeth
   in the crazy metal mouth of night.

THE CUP

Pleased to consider the cup. On a high-up shelf it stands, waiting to be
fingered. Finders keepers. It's its simplicity, to envy. This configuration
of complicity with air, and arms enact handles to tilt it. Roundelay for a sip
and care beneath it, cantankerous baby. Upholds the light in holes, holding in
liquid minutia as though a sister. Or twinned slippers hushing carpet stairs;
four hands with glasses, crown glass with milk and a nipple knob in it.

Cucurbit for the spilly pieces. Pleased to consider the cup. Precisely why
it matters most emphatically. Usufruct of quantities of unknown property. By
which method of doing. If saucers—a dado below in difference. Or blue, for
example. Teethed with crenels like castle turrets, yes.

What I want is to hand around it, insideways often. It hurts less to know its
absence is natural. Pleased to consider. The cup lobs lookingly like honey.

*

So, abandon hope. Of course, it's most natural to want it intact; the crack
from lip to base faces south and south. Smooth lazy susan whirls and twirls so.
But, if it basks in perfection, call it cul-de-sac. Call it caved-in-cup,
spinning—unpleased to consider the consequences of indabbing fingers, which
lose their gloves—minus the digit-mask, like some anemone from the sea.

Enemy is the pace. In which manner of thinking. Space to curl into it.
So pleased! Drink up. To consider most lovingly intonations of refusal, drains
your energy. Gully dint is coming. Bees don't squeeze from honeycomb fumes.
Out back the hat-hive-house stands, pleased to squat in sun—most roundly.
Only to have itself to consider.

*

Enclosed spaces with borders not to be crossed—jimpson fences. So that's
why the bell stings. Orchestrated petals reek havoc in the shade of night.
Sweet and sour pork. Pleased to be sure to lock all doors, to hit the light.
Casuistry says this is the way the gentlemen ride—hippety, then, but, oh—
from toe to heel the campanile shifts, suffering contrecoup. An elegant silence
darkened by sidelighting.

In the cup she puts five things. Today the tides, some crumbs, a lunar key.
The wolf of Gubbio leaves five teeth, a bloody kiss by her negligee. Put them
in, and then ... So what of laughter bouncing within? Intaglioed complaints
brim her blown-glass goblet. What he cups in his hands is neither, nor water.

*

Slip on his hands, the cup grows. Soft underneath, it will harden. *Cunning,*
She says, *touch.* She says: *Massage and mass ... sage ... message ... mess and age ...*
and the cup grows most pleasingly. *Don't touch,* she says—*much, to consider.*

—*for Robert Antoni*

ABOUT REFUSAL

...fear in fear the name the blue and green walls
falling of and numbers fear the veins that
when they were opened fear flowed from and
these forms it took a ring a ring a ring
a bit of grass green swan's down gliding on
fear into fear and the hatred and something
in everything...   —W.S. MERWIN

She stands hands half-submerged in light, half suds,
    hands half incarnadine with blood. What is she
        thinking, what can she think? It flips and slaps
    in the porcelain basin, alive and gasping, if fish
can gasp. How when what matters is only
    this: the mind finally unhands, it man-
        umits in fact, the body, tells it: *Go*
            (burly body)—*Abandon your island,*
    follow the bight's long slow curve always
    inward toward the shackled heart, and then let
go. How, often when a life is most
    pitifully only ampersand be-
        tween your coming and your departure, how
    then this limbo is straddled sometimes by

the mind saying: *Go now and yes, go now*
    and lead that other life instead; have them
        both all at once. He flares her odium,
    even when he's not there. Even moreso.
Go look, says the mind. *Look in the quick mirror:*
    the pupil blazes from its ring of pie-
        bald fire. In the burning kitchen, her small
            soup boils over. She thinks she looks no
    different than when she chose wrong (Oh, years
ago)—so still she wishes she hadn't.
She's drawn to holes rent in the knees, places
    open needing her stitching, sutures she makes to
        tie herself to another. But her torsion gets
    her nowhere further ever than this mind-

less kitchen, the ranging vine, the shadowed
    wall and sunbaked tile. So effortlessly
        she scales and guts, pushing the slick blade in,
    a smooth flick down, to free thick blood—its flow
an easy mockery of children no
    longer children. She loves this fish, packing
        dry fennel lovingly into the space.

What of the vitreous eye (—the fly which
alights)—and albuminous liver? Good
liver; on the ledge it tries to contain
itself near the far edge of the sink, but
keeps slipping in. So, when the sullen man
she despises (yet married) sluices his
heavy hands at the spigot, the silent

liver sits silent in puddle water.
Drunken fly unstitches the silence with
wings hardly visible and zags toward a
screenless window. Go, she thinks. *Go,* says the
mind. *What matters is to hold onto some-*
thing. This could be a dream, for example
this could even be a dream: nondescript
and inhabited by common men she
rarely speaks to but thinks of. And if so,
at the sink she wonders if the breathing
out, if in the breathing at all—she might
lose (even in the dream) everything—in
small particles. Or possibly everything all
at once. Where can it go? The spinning mind says:

Where do you want it to go? We (I
will there to be one, she thinks) *can*
get inside you, anywhere. Iris (I see you, yes)
pimpernel (hiding), *bloodroot,* (my heart waits)
and the mind whispers: *We can get inside*
your waiting.

THE HAND

Oh, massy amulet, handsel me this—a slap—and thus smack life back into me, as at birth—when, end for end the cool-hand doctor snapped me out of a state called bliss, no, nitrogen narcosis—and one I'd grown to love. To whom do you belong? Palmate root of ginger, five of anything—herrings, blood oranges; that bulk of eight to twenty plantains, which naturally divide. Leopold von Sacher-Masoch. The Marquis de Sade?

I watch you lace your punch with rum. These rooms resemble gurgling aquariums, filled with pink-skinned dolphins and turquoise stones. Your guests twirl in among taffy-hued pagodas and glass-spun castles, snitching carpaccio from lacquered rosewood trays.

What to say? What to wear to hide my dorsal fin? Where to begin? You brandish your calumet and yet—no peace in sight. Please slap me once, tonight.

*

Scutcheon, beacon, cairn. You bowl me over. What you touch becomes you, the way wind sculpts scales of a mackerel sky and the sky becomes both at once composed of shifting air and adorned. Handsome mare's-tail. Wedges of devil's egg, so easy to manipulate. Impassioned hearts of artichoke on toastpoint tips. Beluga caviar dyes the fingers blue. Brainchild of a cyborg, all artificial limbs. The vinyl skin. Just something to grab onto.

*

Always moving, you're not easy to describe. It takes tiny tubes of decoupage glue, to slicken away your unique grooves. Tobacco leaves. Certain bundles of watercress.

Your fillip is quick. Cream streams below the clipped box hedges. Your single hand unlocks me. The nails are smooth and clean. You're all semaphore, and I want more. Small sets of needle-nosed pliers. Flitches of bacon and hands, four grains of barley to a finger. Applause, applause. Help me, Valentina Tereshkova. The gelding stands twelve hands high, stamping a hoof, swishing his mane from his eyes. Let's go riding. Braid me with ribbons and stick me with pins. Your voice wafts over me, silts in my mind, confectioners' sugar like Paris Green, insidious insecticide in wind, and nowhere near to hide.

*

Four braised carrots and a thumb. Your friends are kleptomaniacs, filching checkers from your closet floors. The company we keep. So unsuspecting? After hours we open all the doors and beasts trip in. My cheek burns. The hand glows. It rises in the east each time you strike me.

Vengeful fury—fickle-handed fiasco in its straw-woven crib. How many places do you bend? Extended, you're a bird—pinned against a fiery cross. Cresset, flagstaff, burgees half-mast. Knockdown puffs off Good Hope bluff. Leave the kiss for Lucky Lindy. Leave the lucky hand inside.

*

You read my brow like Braille. You furl me like a sail. You fill my junket mind with cacographic snippets I forget. Unlikely nimbi flare above your knuckles. You toss your bamboo sandals toward the pool. Vouchsafed angel,

I won't tell. I'm a blue wire, sparking in the boulevards. Touch me. I'm an Alsatian husky—tugging at your lead. Don't hold back your loose hand. You flip my switches not against my wishes. Negligence? Not only—clothed me in this beryl negligee.

A ravening desire for your fingers on my skin. Hit me, again. I'm alive.

THE WHITE ISLAND

There is an island she always dreams of, but if ever she arrives, already she wants
        to come back. Up
and down the sea coast she wanders gathering pieces of glass, bones, and papers
        into an ever-changing
tower, hoping one day it will reach the moon. Inside driftwood she finds it is so white
        it is blue like milk,
like the inside of a shape made by bones. And smooth. This whiteness brings tears
        to her eyes. A white like that
of the sea where the sun strikes it cresting, the white pebble beaches, the idea of white
        peaches—fruit from Talouse
which she gathered once for a slim, smooth-skinned man who never showed up. Or
        was he in a dream?

Stucco walls stand like stale cakes and the plumpening grapes climb them with gnarled
        fingers. She shields her
eyes from the brightness knifing like spite, though it will mean bottles to look at, come
        fall. *Pineau des Charentes.*
Something to think. She has returned to her kitchen window, her white porcelain sink
        filled with scales, fins
and the blood of the fish just caught by the man who is not the famous doctor in Paris, is
        not the one who returned from
abroad after two years to find her already married, is not the one she loved to sit with
        in the grand concert hall,
who spoke about Mozart, Pessoa, Marc, Chagall, no. White cows lurch beyond the far
        wall, but no, that is laundry,

white sheets she has laundered, has hung to dry—white sheets bleached and bleached
        in bitter salts to rinse them of
blood spilled not from desire, but fear. He makes her open and close her legs around
        his body so many
nights she grimaces just thinking about his fish cold skin under the duvet with her.
        She rinses the scales from her
knife, sets the sieve of cheese to drain in the sink, *fromage blanc* . . . Milk off ice.
        And the rooster cocks a gravelling
cry she remembers sounding something like that of a woman in childbirth. This pain of
        someone far off, white like
the scorching sand, or so white it is clear, like sambuca or rum from Antigua, that
        burns a clean path down her

throat. Why did she follow this one south, let him take her hands in his rough ones?
        She knits her fingers together,
fingers no longer tapered and pale but weathered like his, fingers adept at stripping
        meat from bones, at snapping
beans, at unscrewing stiff rusted lids from big jars of *confit*, heavy with thick yellow-
        white grease melted once and

now hardened, a bit like her heart. Oh, how she prepares his meal, setting it all at his
place. And with what vengeance
she tears up crisp lettuce, adding so much oil, so much burning vinegar, mustard, salt,
lemon, and thyme, so much as everyone
wants! She arranges his cheeses, the blue porcelain dish of cold artichoke hearts.
She saws lengths from the limblike

baguette, crumbs feather across the cloth. And he begins to shovel his food, without
comment, even before
she has pulled out her chair. He never waits. *Why didn't I wait?* she worries, *for
Docteur S.* How different
her life would be. *Champagne, papillon,* she thinks of pretty words and watches
this other swallow his food. *If
you choose not to come along, I can't promise there will be another chance . . .* this plays
through her mind like an
annoying musical strain. The choices she has to make even daily, on the beach—
which green glass to keep,
which tangled piece of wood. She concentrates on her book of photographs, kept in the
oak cabinet with the cups and

plates, her mother's *armoire de chene.* She knows its scent by heart, and the smooth
feel of the book stuffed
with scallop-edged shots of a man and woman, married twelve years before her birth—
her parents, happy in the
Pyrenees, caught in little scenes, here in a field, here by plashing white falls, pieces
of sunlight and shade,
black arches ducked under to kiss. She considers what kissing once was like—what
she has missed. *Yes.*
And the island she dreams of. And always a *Docteur S.,* the set of his eyes, his hands,
his lower lip, his voice—
tipped from a moon-round goblet, his quicksilver hair, his moving through rooms some-
where.

THE SPOOL

You didn't say. This intense necessary inside. Feathers off, un-
wind please to pose upside his easel. Teflon electrons. Limicoline
living. Your toothy cutlass grin. You narrow fish—dismembered
for spinning. Insalubrious palette, inklings in cephalic zones.
Stones with holes and spindles with rims. He found that by the sea.

You didn't say. This scabrous filament of fuschia. Cunctation
hurts, you know. Your clinging sea-oak limbs and sweet japonica
wilts. Now, the wish is plumose, falling lightly like nightly light.
That tongue fits with practice. Cactus needles prick, and sails
go spuming—how many years ago how so, before the wind. Unwind.

You didn't say. This turbinado sugar blows like sorrow, blows
like spite. Inside I hide, a cuttlefish corolla spewing ink, while
others think I'm nothing. You're returning for the wear. Black air
my caring calyx. Taunting, teasing kitty, you dance around me, clad
in gingerbread pants. Whose languor legs once over, tether wrapped.
Sanguinaria . . . scattered on the limen. Ask me why.

*

I can't forgive you. Subtle mesh entangled. Go on, and go on.
Screw your thimble thumbward. Unforgiving, what's left outside by my
umbrageous laughter. Tides flood in and often. Latent maelstrom—
buried deep within. And your pretty streaming. And your endless
winding. I can't because I'm hollow. Forgive my pensive shadow.

I can't because you're hollow.

Subtle how we're one, and how enraptured. How all is tangled
round my wooden ribbing. How you are riant in your saying: *This.*

This, miss . . . Miss this because of beauty, this. And kissing
also. Flaxen thread above the shoulders, smothers doing. Hovers
longer. Almond outer begs attention, boasts in smoking silk and
leather. Hurtful skirt eclipsing pleasure. You're his mother.

If you're hollow. How I hate you.

*

Turbination in a cauldron. Puzzled with nucleic acid. Threaded
steam makes mere embroidery—embouchure of flowing, hardly knowing
what we're doing. Fancifully embellish boredom. In this kingdom,
what's the spool?

29

You didn't say, and that's my rule. You didn't say.

*

All inside you. Necessary. All outside me. Necessary.

Ask me why.

Running off around that other, harboring his transom hands. Wooden
lover, lathed together. Pinions clipped despite the breeze. Salty
kippers, lipping malice. Whirring in a practiced turning, you try
splitting from your past—leaving it, abandoned troche, bullet
nestled in the sand. False gyrations in defense. Doubting ritual
defervescence, and the coolness of this spool. I wait spinning—
hand to hand.

*

You didn't say. This pleasing limit of utility. Silent bobbin,
dimpled ribbon. When you're strung out, you come back. Doused in
meretricious oils, layers of it which never dry. Ask me, and I'll
tell you why:

When the tube is spent up finished, in my hardness I will last.
Basking in centripetal granite. Tempered inward avalanche.

BREAKFAST: THE BOY EINSTEIN

1

Her from herself to disentangle were she able. Two
birds on the sheet called hands. Mine, she thinks, *Me.*

And that which leaps invincible through the panes.
That which moves in ways not yet acknowledged. First, only
that he too exist.

Rim of a frayed wool collar blacker than
the room's corners still unbathed
by light, rolled back to give a voice a solid surface, between
clavicle and mandible, emerges from them. It's him.

2

Her effort forms in a graceful curl. One foot over.
Like a yolk scooped with a spoon, that which rises outside her, spills
over and fills her with a warmth akin to company. Transport such as this
occurs invisible. Once partial
both to air and sea, the body of a flying
fish lies quiet on a platter glazed with copper. Its scales though useless
currency, still shining.

3

How then can she move about the table. What describes a circle on the gingham is
his finger, slowly. His halo strikes her heart before she hears him. *Hello,* saying it.

4

Could he know then what he was making possible? Agent
of her being more than body, his small body taking shape
within her mind. Tousled, tripping lightly down
her stairs. What she has him think, has him carry. Schoolbooks,
yes. Her geometry: a frail line finally connecting drops of
milk, drilling the pail. Anatomy: cross sections of pink fruits with nubbled skins
peeled back. Four plump seeds cradled in flesh. All glistening, all waiting to burst.

And what severed by what had to follow was her desire, from her knowing.
That she was singular in her seeing she could feel.
He materialized in the morning like a dove which seemed
a silver bloom, dropped gently from the limbs of an acacia. Long named
internal bleeding, made most visible

5

but, that she chooses to disregard it.

Something so easy to will and pleasing, now gives her the freedom to act

without entirely singular consideration. At least . . .
Two forks, two cups, all pairs; though, were someone to see: only one
pair of lungs pulls in the air, expels the air.
Something musical about the arched back of the chair itself. The boy,
an implied adjective. The shape she leaves, being
precisely equal to her size. Or slightly greater.

6

Always, she moves as if beckoned by a boy. Hours all
but standing still. A seldom woman knocking
with a basket of berries or eggs. *Talk talk. Stop over, anytime.*

After-what, Why-now, Any-when. The others, later
whisper: *she's gone
a bit strange. . . .*

What slides along the casement, waiting to fix her

7

exactly *here,*
as it sweeps across the floor, as she sweeps the corners,
contributes to the continuum of seconds and planes.
How two outdoors can weave a seat of arms for a third to climb
up onto, then be carried. She remembers as a child.
A second muffin from the basket better for being
wiped with butter, crumbles slightly in his hand, *her* hand. Blood-
orange pulp thickens the glass's rim in minutes. She sees them:
tick *tick* of the red hands. Lips daubed with linen. Every finger licked in ceremony.

8

And yes. The result of his prayed for presence, a warping of her
quiet morning in a way quite parabolic. So that her body moving both
through stone-floored halls and thin-aired hours actually approaches
a kind of near perfection. Her twirling slowly. Calm face now caught
in the ancient mirror as she rounds a corner. *Me,* she thinks. Still falling
into the idea of it. Sun-warmed fruit, dropping
into an upturned palm. *The important thing is not to stop
questioning.* Rolling it over in her mind. Brushing the bloom away. *Echo,
echo* on the night-chilled stones. Dust swirling behind. Rubbing sleep
from the lashes of the eyes she dreams for him. The shimmer
which is the idea of him. The parer like a language
on her skin. Beyond this surface, outside
the glass, green blades rise through a net of light—light falling and caught
in each small world of water balanced there. And someone
to share this silence . . . And see it. See it and *feel it.*
The rasp an edge of dampened cloth
would make, taken firmly
to his blushing cheek, and with pleasure.

THE RUFFLED EDGE

Smoked salmon leather, this thong of a man, who ambles by water in a directed south
      saunter over gravelly
sand—now wet purple where it rims the sea. He carries an oblong sack his own
      skin's color. His plastic
shoes, clear with numerous holes (*sloosh in sloosh out*) make a squelching sound. She
      lifts her head, ball-
bearing pivot, to widen her peripheral range; he knows she's there and he figures
      she sees him; cap bobbing
blue like dark water. She lies beneath dunes amidst shells—curled in glass eye
      colors. Sand rises in wind,
creamy and sorrel. Ka-plunge *plunge*—dog feet in shallows sends a crawl up the salt-
      pulled skin on her spine.

Sun prisms hot shards, and black dots squabble, moaning and mewing in thin air. She
      follows him, eyes tracing his
lines—the path of his all-one-color skin, as he wanders. Wound tight rubber-bands
      and a rounded nub hangs in front,
while his legs just continue. Up in back too, merely darker. Ribs she can see and his
      bones through his skin, weathered
parchment, shell of a valuable book, striated ink, marbled like smoked rump of a pig
      been skinned. How common this
hairlessness, she thinks, thinking: how I should write that *here*, held in a purple
      cup, headside toward bluffs, feet
pointing down across the Atlantic toward ... America?—(she stretches her body in
      length toward some green

grey seaport on the eastern coast, maybe Boston, maybe even the wharf with that big
      hotel. She spent the night
with a man buying drinks with so many pieces of money it began way past dark, to
      resemble useless,
dirty handled roughage of paper, lettuce promises which wilted, as the evening wore
      on, while he
all the time, heated up; his coins clacked angrily like bits of glinty glass in the sea
      of melted ice and foam
at the bar, chips worn deceptively smooth from his shifty use, but oh-so-dangerously
      brittle, algid, sharply insincere and ...)
—that: It's good. Something at least. Small rise of sand, size of one hand, by her
      navel. And lower.

She watches him pass, tipping the frame of her rib cage forward, and he, still passing
      below her, halts; they're
somehow together. What would the others say if they came down to the beach where
      she rocks—her excitement
too much to contain—and she could feel herself swell, like the dark blue water, swell
      in their sight, save
for the blood-black interior, the elastic smooth eel-kush-hibiscus bruising interior of her
      favorite flower—which is

always in bloom, or can be on command, and is, therefore, often the favorite. And
    then she lies back
hearing the bubbled muskiness of the sea; sun climbs high over whispering grass, reeds,
    vetch and thistle, spikegrass

and wheat. *Kasherrr kashush*—the plashings of low surftide into reefs lull her, a
    gentle breakage. Thinking:
dizzy gazing down waterway of algae green like frog green soup swamp stubble growth
    of reef bone clean sticks of carnage . . .
Heat soaks through. On her skin she feels a double-tone horn somewhere, a single
    noise. And far off a rumble purr.
The bubbling motor of an aeroplane, red-white toy pulled bobbingly across the enamel
    blue, clay-baked cloudless
sky. Sea a bit darker rising in caps, catches her eye, just before closing. She
    imagines walking
over the dune-cliff edge toward: the harbor, stands selling rounds of ice cream in bright
    colors, seafoam green

shutters, high blue trees and blue pink shadows, toward glinting stucco, brilliant orange
    pink red green purple black fishing
boats, dune-pink buildings—their green and white awnings striped over tables with tiny
    wire chairs set in rings, over
grasses, cobbles, near benches, tar and creosote in her nose, warm black on her feet
    and bonfire air, good sharp
salt air, toward the red light on the point, vinegar light in the house saying—watch
    out here, past boats docked for lunch
of fish and baguettes, yellow-suited men in their curls and caps with tins, clinking
    bottles, melting colors
in the water, toward cafés under awnings, bow-tied, box-coated waiters, yawning in the sun
    on the terrace, suit jackets double-

breasted grey with four buttons done up, down by the hips, spit-polished
    men asking—what
would she like. What would she like? What she would like *is . . .*
    and she opens her eyes.
He is merely a shape, arms-legs-bag dangling down darkening in the center, hollowing
    in the rear, smooth contoured
like clay, whelk of a shell, conch of a cake of a lifetime. He stops slowly, stands, toes
    in the water's frill, pivots
360 degrees, from his kidney bean sack he extracts a small stripe of turquoise cloth,
    two boys wail by in bright
short pants. *How far is it?* to some (unknown) destination . . . Two more voices and a
    third approach—and he once nude

now steadies himself, lifts first his right then left leg through spaces meant for legs,
    and all most gingerly completed,
he moves off, shifting from pale stone to stone, his spine growing more distant but
    concurrently seeming sharper

on the horizon, a mahogany nick, a nut or vessel, easing away, his blue stripe blue no
    more but seeping to be
his color, hangs low on his hips, torso long letting his suit slip to reveal the top of
    dividing buttocks, dark space
peeping above color, more pleasing … She lets go. It feels good, this, that
    particles spin and she brushes the skin
on her arms as though to rub it away and suddenly she decides to tear up the card she
    had written before, stuck in her
book to mail on the way, addressed in green ink to some other who mattered, who is, as
    it happens, covered with a forest

mat of dark hair, curled like fur of the dog in the surf, some man in a city where
    pressed shirts are required, where
sand is a tiring nuisance, and dunes can't possibly hide what goes on, and furthermore,
    stretching to stand
she unfolds toward the clear flat open expanse of sky, walks gingerly also, yet with
    confidence toward the incoming
onrushing waves. It seems to take her forever, she thinks. *How long have I been*
    walking directly toward this—
impossible distance. Just when she has decided to stop, *ah*, she's arrived at the ruffled
    edge. She tears the card with its

glossy view and its spindly message into tiny triangular pieces and *Whoosh*, she lets go.
    They scatter … wafting away, small sails
capping the waves, some ripple over the horizon where America probably still hunkers,
    some drift up toward Concarneau and
Penzance, then on to St. Georges Channel and Newcastle, then even past Ireland all
    together, and the Hebrides and off toward Iceland
and maybe even further past that … and there are others which swirl down toward San
    Sebastian, riding the currents which stir
the Bay of Biscay, making their way out and around Spain's shoulder, buoyed off toward
    Portugal, Tangier, into the Mediterranean Sea
toward Italy, then Cyprus, following currents through the Dardanelles, past Istanbul,
    eddying into the Black Sea, and then …

III

FUGUE

True, they are not at rest yet,
but now that they are indeed
apart, winnowed from failures,
they withdraw to an orbit
and turn with disinterested
hard energy, like the stars.
—THOM GUNN

I.

As when the potter, seduced by slip, leans
into the soft mouth he fingers
with all his heart, presses
the spinning earth
between his hands, spends
it all while it's what
he's got . . . too hard, and punctures
the growing pot—*No*, you say.
No wasted love. Though your tongue
has become a dead vole,
small in a corner you hoped
would brighten. Simple words spoken
so slowly they're
indiscernible. Keep the wheel
turning, always in the same direction.
And then that drip again
singing: *But   but   but   but . . .*

Whose souls are borne off in these fractured
jars. Whose shoulders bear such weight and how far
must they go. I who walk the rutted streets
hardly letting my silver heels touch,
I have already begun a secret journey. Either pollen
or ash stains the air like a carnallite shadow more
visible than its object. Six golden amphorae
tease the sun. Riva,
                            the swell of your hipbone leads me
down into a place sopping with hope and confusion. Only
when lank light slips through your parted
blinds, will I collect my unraveling green sweater
and leave with the taste of you still
on my face and hands.

Don't concern yourself with accurate
dates and specific places. This is a film all shot
somewhere else some other time. It's *real*, man. Trust
me. Or, concern yourself—all's shot; show's over.

Another voice whines, did I dance in the lower left

39

corner of light, back on the second reel? And finally,
who is that small blonde child playing
the part of the sorcerer's apprentice, the one scooping
and bailing invisible water through gaseous air,
casting it there, over the transfixed attendants
and why don't they actually feel the spray
when the bowl clangs down?

Lead me to the glowing kiln
and balance me within on plaster bats. Riva, my heart
of quickened terra cotta sloughs in the fire. I lie,
even as the question is asked. I describe intricate plots
of films I've never seen. I nod a lot and display
my passive agreement.

But I will not die like that.
Help me, if you are able; we don't have time to kill
in the luxurious manner of bankers, monied and slick, on
weekends away in Sagaponack. The end
is inescapable. How many have tested sick?
And once the house lights go down,
only the exit signs burn. We meet beneath door frames
in a string of ignited places, torched
from the air, as if a necklace of stars
seeded below the outstretched wings we ride on.
I would fly anywhere for the right one. *Some quiet*

aberration, mistaken for profundity.
Anywhere, wincing. Whether
we grow more valuable for duration. *Or?*
Fireworks. The walls rise
higher, the wheel spins on. Wider ...
stick your hands in, the leather
clay opens, spins, *desire,*

climbs higher, drips
down the wrists, then buckles
and folds.   How ungodly tired
I think we must be ...

We should be
like animals, mating for life.

Have you ever
been in that position, waiting for month's
end? Happy accidents, Riva. Though
the simple pleasure of buttered toast,
the familiar tide of your inner
weather and mine aligning, with time. ...
Still, a thrill for uncharted water

sends me out toward the water's rim.

Across the sea, I once claimed the early stairway
of San Paolino for myself, I claimed
the wide steps up, I claimed the sun and watched

the world roll with it—up, skidding over fat walls
across the gleaming labor-stricken faces, the tiered dark
buildings, light rising along the cakelike lines
of architectural structures no longer seen
the likes of . . .
                    Why do we build
            a world of ruin around us, if that is what we fear?
Light pours through cypress almost violently, a commerce
of leaves, a halo for the poor
saints, condemned by Filippino Lippi to live
their days, witnesses to the ways of those who cherish
the ruins we wreak by living. From each alcove, wide
gargoyled eyes spurt baptismal waters
                              on all of us below who cannot hide.

            Why is it that I never pleased him,
            Or was it, pleased myself?
            On the day of his funeral
            where will I be? Pitching pebbles
            into a can with no label,
            dangling bread crumbs
            for the fattened fish, no doubt.
            How, for example, there
            beside us on the stand
                                    under the window
            by the bed, the deflated drippings of our love
have dried in yellow rings like amber
beer—sticky and probably sweeter
than when spilled
but no longer something to ingest.

                            II.

            This world's a mess. I count the men my friend
                        has been with and multiply by ten times ten
            times ten and ad infinitum. *My sad captains.*

My wodded sadness. They swallow themselves,
the years and centuries, coiling mouth to tail so
12th rolls into 21st while I'm not looking.
But feel the shudder. From the loggia,
one in black silk trousers trills:
                        you cannot kill us all
                        merely by shooting yourself. Yellow jackets
                        swarm about his head, as if his lips dripped
                        honey. All eyes roll upward.

            In the barber's mirror
            an old man from the *pensione*, lathered up, eyes
            closed, waits woolly-jowled for the blade
            to cross his throat. Sheep in the hands of others,

41

bleatless in perplexed fear at the smell of death
spurting before them, blood thick in the folds
of necks, the blue-black silence, the screamingness
of mutual blaring pain. And then,

it's over . . .
        Why do I move
through this world with blinders on?
I want to throw myself
around some dumb and matted friends;
I want to stop the river of their blood.
For what do sheep count,
as they line up mutely for this unwanted
final sleep . . .
                Please, count me.

            The trees beyond the walls
            hold up their arms in mimicry
            of candelabras. I watch, at Pasticceria Pasquinelli, as
            sugar falls from elaborate pastries, the dusting of
            chocolate into cups of chocolate, while grates
            roll up, continually giving birth
            to storefronts, and somewhere after nine
            the world's emerged. I'm frightened, Riva, of the pain
            you already know from having given

birth, not so much the bloody ripping
but rather, the letting go. With my fingers
just resting beside you, we drift toward sleep
and somehow
my fear disperses. In a dream,

                    flashback to Kutztown . . . Straddling
            his neck. Prickly heat. I rode above all
            on my father's shoulders, between festooned stands
            where costumed men together made
            pinwheels and chairs carved for giants and others
            shoed horses.
                        When he lifted me off, the zoomed-
in world rocked beneath my feet, lurched and made me reel like the rum on his breath
looked like frog eyes underwater and I hid behind that blue door until he came back
through the rain with sodden paper plates of mincemeat shoofly pie horse-corn on
the cob swabbed with butter stuck to my chin in bits here let me wipe you off and
honeycomb the chaff flying his laughter almost frightening beeswax candles dripping
stalactites while jingling oxen shouldered yokes against one another and a barn-raising
got under way its walls just rising sideways in one synchronized pull of their hands and
at the end
            my head spinning, cheeks burning,
                        feet aching, my crying . . . we arrived
at the slaughterhouse. It's all
wound up together. Thin hairs of blood-
tinged saliva drape their patterned

web still in my mind from
the fleshy lips of steer, their grizzled coats
and marbleized mambo eyes. Riva, if this
were a scene from *Madame Bovary*
would you choose to cut back and forth
from the bargaining voices below to the sighs
of love above in the rafters?

                Perhaps it is only necessary to hear
                glottals and jabs, the jovial
                bantering of rising prices, punctuated
                by canvas-thick punches...
                tonal backdrop for the scene at hand.

Some linguistic rationale. I learned
about perspective while in school
but somehow, when the alley closes in around me
I forget its logic, its meaning of vectors leading
toward a pin of light I hope to find
as tangible as nouns. And yet
I never reach it. By the sea, fine grains of sand
converge, reflecting light in such a way
at the far end of the earth's smooth bight, I could
climb up it, ascend the pillar, rise
like the surmounting archangel Michael, through a geometric
field of intricate plumery—animals and flowers, entwined
below a brilliant blankness above. But no,

                the world straps down my ankles, sucks me
                in. The cobbler, Crispin,
                saunters down the via di Poggia, October 25th and winks
                at all the barefoot girls. The heavy-lidded boys loiter
                before their lessons. A woman leans to hang
                wet shirts two floors above, sleeves rolled on her olive
                arms, elbows raw red scuffed. Her green and yellow
                shutters flung to air
                the room of sleep, absorb the sun. Her lips
                a bow-tied apricot of light. She's singing to herself.
                The news has not yet arrived. Not yet her news. No one

has died
yet, and if one could freeze her here forever,
no one would.
Don't tell her. It hasn't happened
if she doesn't know.

III.

                Be thankful for the harvest. This day
                the Benediction of Tractors fills the square,
                mute yellow hulks tethered in the cobbled pasture. All come
                bearing gifts. Farmers and vintners, a blonde child, a mother,

merchants of silks, bakers of bread, the potter
and one who blows glass. Nobody is last
before the eyes of our father.
                                                Phone lines hang
between steeples and jails, quivering in howling wind
which tunnels the smog; they crisscross unseen, sharp
as blades of twine suspended for the unavoidable,
inevitable decapitation of our movie's hero. My mother,

        if only then I could have asked her:
What is it about me? How
can I stay young and yet outgrow
the britches of a past we've worn together,
shedding one snakelike skin
in a baking sun, without contempt?

I would offer anything
to have a second chance; the boy-
shaped ginger cookies I cut and bake each
December, are as close to Balder's effigy
as I can manage. Sometimes
the raisin eyes burn, but blackened
sugar is sweetest
and carbon cleans the teeth. Her voice

                    goes through me as does Riva's. Only in the afterstun
                    when I've placed the smooth synthetic cowry
                    in its plastic cradle and am alone again
                    do I realize just how alone I am. Pathetic voice. Starving
                    and crazed, the tapeworm smelling a musky steak, drags
                    itself up and out, not sensing death, drawn out
                    by a quiet voice of a beast
                    it hears in hers. A beast, which lying coiled becomes both
                    ballast and a curse.

Another woman—raging at a man beneath her
in a small fenced courtyard with swung-open gates,
flaps red sheets against lemon stucco,
and spits. Across the mall
a pink wall bleeding rust screams silently
in smeary green graffiti *Noli me tangere*
and then beside in black, a heart
painted at heart height and pierced.
                            Below, heaps
of debris gather in the crease where wall meets
stone, large loaflike presences soiled
wet in patches. The village dog sniffs his way
around the square. Here,

            lightning flashes more like lost strobes in Manhattan clubs
                    than anything else I've found

44

out on the prairie, igniting the quiddity
of any moment between
two unfamiliar people. For example
this moment—when the middle-aged woman with dirty
feet, unfolds
her papers and begins telling
poems. Suddenly I remember:
Shhhhhhhhh,
whispers the sea,
from a very long way off.

And Riva's voice as underscore:
You don't need all the *maquillage,*
Wipe it off!

Please, help me
accept who I have been and grown
to be. Please grow too
and do not yet die
as all my friends are dying.
The surf pulls back, then
belches forth a froth of razored stone.

A wafer sucks the moisture
from the tongue of a man
sweating in the foyer. His hand slips deep into his pocket.

One voice together says: *Spiritus Sanctus.*

The clink of coins pressed by blackened hands
through slots, rings in the temple
of each mind hoping to be bathed of sin.
Near the door the man steals
a peek over his shoulder. His wife
wears her hair most heavily, the weight of it increasing
with his lies. Her eyes grow daily
more opaque. Two dark and uninhabited stars. She is rising
from her body. The excess bulk of her, the heft
of calves once shapely, now passed, drips from her
like the pooling wax of candles, candles flickering
from every nook like flashing eyes of the slender girls
he can't resist. *But,*

but their time will come, she thinks
sinking into a sadness shared by all who see
an imminent collapse, a gravitation into rubble.
Voice-over: *We will implode this ball in time.*
Each chiming of the bells erases years.

What a thing to think;
what a thing to think is.
And somewhere, after all, another world

45

exists. I tell myself. How
in the neon smear of light
a burning rain pelts down on streets
awash in Chinatown, and then
somewhere between Broome and Spring,
it stops
and everything glistens
with the fluorescence of newborn mice
radiant in its hideousness:
the blind man who stands for hours in darkness
trying repeatedly to set
his lawn chair out, as though there may still be a sun
to worship when he's done, despite
the legs all broken inward, the slats worn through—
even he is jeweled and lovely to behold . . .

IV.

I am worrying the water with my tires.
And all
here in this mosaic of night,
all my actions here in darkness
resemble an illusive sciamachy
conducted for the pleasure of children
there, before the scrim.
I seek
not beautiful men, but rather
those with women like exotic birds perched near,
women whose mouths spread
into wide bowls of ivory, whose wet eyes
are almond-shaped and always moving,
whose names are many syllabled and often end in 'a.'

The gesture hangs above them like
fine ocean spray.
                    . . . and the fighters
behind the crates, one down
encircled in glittering
bits of glass, his mother's tears
perhaps, pomegranate blood, lurid and
pavonine and beautiful beyond compare—
some young Adonis, ennobled by the boar, sweet
anemone, spiked flower bending in this blunt
instrument, wind of both creation and decay.
And there, by the cars, the one
who checks for radios
though everyone knows no one leaves
them anymore, here
in the city, and if they do—they deserve it.

They surge in and out, disappearing in the undertow.

46

Already, it was much too late to save us, Riva, even
before I set out to tell this; and this,
the first decisive move I've made, already
it is wrong. I let your milk drops
seep into my curled-up straw paper and it unfurls deliberately
like a trained white worm.
                                                Winged mice
skim the night sky, and suddenly I, too, understand their
radar songs. Draw back the blood-
red velvet curtain, lift up these vinyl waves; strip away
the chalky skin. In a bistro lit
only by the flickering TV, you are
free to choose any available girl, but
I suggest either the sable-eyed singer at the bar or
the albino with the tellurium bod, crouched near that corner
table. She's fifteen. Out back, the offal
cast to a pack of snapping curs
resembles something I once found—

by the sea, a green
trash bag, loosely tied but torn
spilling a mass of carcass, the rib cage of none
other than a man. I could tell, the entrails,
lungs.
          I left it there, fearing not
that which had inflicted such a foul
demise, but rather
a daunted world in which I could just witness
such monstrosity and wander on.
I am a beast. I kick the sand.
My foulness eats inside me like a sea;

already sacks of eggs, pouches
of brine and life had sloshed
into the crevices, already gnats had glued
themselves to ragged pieces of decaying flesh
and over all, shadows fell. My bone cage
will not hold such nausea always; constantly
I cast a hand out for a rail, feeling
the planet heel up horizontally
on the massive wake of something speeding by.
Salt stings in my eyes.
                              Her eyes.

Their wedding was a clip from some old movie.
Her uncle with his horse-hands straddled the altar to capture
another best shot, a close-up of her eyes, those
of a trapped animal, black currents in the whiteness of her
face, a sheet of pastry already seeping oil in the hospital
light, already pasty. This beginning was her end.
The mouth, its pulling corners, tells stories

no one wants to hear, though one voice toward the back
wailed: *I object.* But no.

She drifted down the aisle as on ice, projecting
　　　her dim horror toward such fate. In fact she seemed
　　　　　to crave it, going to it like one who feels
　　　　　　she's lucky, fortunate enough
　　　　　　　　to escape without succumbing first to cancer of, say,
　　　　　　　　　　the breasts.　　As though she had made it
　　　　　　without getting something awful, painful, bleak, made it
　　　　　　and been healthy and had thereby won out, by dying
　　　　　　without having first died.
　　　　　　　　　　　　Riva, she cries
　　　　　years later but her tears
　　　　　will not be heard.
The projector pushed too close to the gel film burns the image out
but sears it in our brains.
The only plot progression
is the one we run through
in our minds.
Our lids descend.
We settle in our bodies,
play these scenes
we conjure anywhere
at any time. *Cross cut*　　　　　　　to another scene, again
　　　　　　　　　　　　　　between Spring and Broome, one with
　　　　　　　　　　　　　　Jael and Sisera, one of conventional
　　　　　　　　　　　　　　slow-motion violence. And domesticity. What need,

V.

Riva, for verbs when at her feet he
bowed, he fell, he lay down: at her feet
he bowed, he fell and where he bowed, there
he fell down dead . . .
and his mother, wringing her sticky hands
and his mother, seeping her vinegar tears
and his mother, somewhere outside the circle of
streetlights looks up from her simmering
curry, his mother, bathed frail yellow
by the single naked bulb,
looks out through the lattice, *why*
is his chariot so long in coming—
have they not sped?
　　　　　　　　　　The head of the crowbar rings
　　　　　　　　　　near the wheel of his junked-up Chevy
　　　　　　　　　　like starch-caked aluminum bowls
　　　　　　　　　　slung into Mama's sink on a busy night. *So let*
　　　　　　　　　　thine enemy perish. This leaking faucet
　　　　　　　　　　some Jack tries to patch, speaks to tomato-stained cups
　　　　　　　　　　crowding the sink: *but　　but*

48

but let them that love him be as the sun. Rising,
rising. But Riva, they're dying. We have to stop
them from dying. Last call
at one o'clock, and then rising
up baffled, we all swim home through rings
of pearl smoke. After nearly thirty years
one acquires sea legs of sorts.
Then at odd moments
in some borrowed shower on land
the Ferris wheel lurches up, up and higher—
its tired metal spokes
groaning and pinging, the grease-stained
straps cutting into my child-
pink thighs, my eyes stuck wide open
and tracking the awkward conniptions of far-off
ants below, the fat domed roofs
of carnival tents, bright flags slapping
the popcorn breeze, my hair wrenched back, *hover*
hover…my stomach
now hollow, then
                    over

                         again. Once back
                         from some sea voyage, I breathe
                         relief. My anchor's cast. All the rigging lights
                         brush and whisper
                         in a lost
                         language, so simple yet
                         swan-elegant it is not unlike
                         that of stars, full
                         of curvature and sibilance
                         and a clarity that almost hurts.

                         As when I leaned to touch silver
                         in the graveled sand. O, muzzy
                         mole, star-nosed, bloody-snouted blind and dusty
                         potato by the curb, forgive me. I find myself
                         forever crashing through underbrush,
                         crushing the tiniest most vivid
                         violets and pinks—but unable
                         to tread any more lightly. And nightly,

I dream I am running up a slope of caved-in sand
with the back of some slightly familiar
compactly built man
always just disappearing ahead of me.
Once he is gone, we cannot bring him back.
I dream beneath constellations of rabbits and dogs
about the piazza San Michelle:
the lean torsos and haunches
of beasts, now life-
less meat, hanging skinned in long divided bodies

like some anatomy lesson I never quite learn—
eyes of some, glazed
like those of the handcuffed hood, bathed
in his brother's blood. Forever silent brother
speak to me?

VI.

               When we wake, Riva, I hear the neighbor's dog.
               The way he gums the piece of meat-bone,
               globs of pink—gunked in his blue-black mane, the way
               he juggles it all—bounces it in his jawclamps like a prized
               dead bird, before finding the softest touch
               to carry it off beneath a tree,
               to snarl later at Lydia who's almost
               two, who wobbles close to pet both bone and dog,
               not knowing the difference between
               the two—and really, what difference is there?
               Once he is gone....
               So wasteful....
               But....
                     but, the potter lifts his dripping hands
               and with a sudden rush,
               he lets them drop
               to wedge another ball. And the wheel spins round.

Riva, come shake the sleep
from your matted hair and watch black
coffee drip into the glass carafe
with me in this city where the fruit is not
seasonal but always opulent, berries
like globes waiting to be crushed
when brushed against by legs moving too fast . . .
sickly, sweetly, redolently reeking in the hazy
sun, a grime silt settling there even
as the aproned grocer mops, the greasy window
cracked behind the fruit stand
where they crouch in wooden crates
cupping light, quelching in the fingers, on the lips,
fingers and lips staining, full as though to burst
with blood, each tiny sack . . .
               all circles back, you see. These knots
               all glowing coded color
               flare our desire once
               again to speak to one another without
               words—like quipu messages
               sent over thousands of centuries and miles
               of sand, braided letters
               passed hand to hand from some hopeful
               other world. The potter's fingers tingle,
               as do mine as I lean into Riva

to stroke the fine silt
of her hair. In the yard below, a boy

Jack? his hands full of magic beans
stands at the foot of a giant stalk, not knowing
whether to shift his weight up
onto his uplifted leg again, or better
just run and hide. The sun bakes down on his horse-wide
shoulders, and always a small breeze teases
him into believing
his climb to a coolness above
will be brief . . .
I'll leave him
there deciding.

VII.

The fattened fish I haven't caught
loll in their goldness under thin black ice,
some silent moment a season
away. And if I could just stop
the turning
page where it stands between *once*
and *then*, here by holding the cold hands
of the mindless clock,
stuck on the wall above the stove . . .

If I could freeze the bullet
somewhere midair
before it spiders the plate-glass pane,
and halt the cresting
wave at its peak
guarding the dunes from the sucking tides,
and pin these rides to the carnival sky
keeping the screaming and falling at bay
and suspend the plinking
drip in flight, staving that inevitable intrusion

of doubt, and keep the blade
from puncturing through, the pressing
fingers stroking the clay, and in that moment while my heart
burns like a fire, eating a wild magenta moon
at the unbroken rim of horizon fields,
I will lock pale eyes with the man on the street, with
a horse swimming there in a pasture of rye, with the woman a thousand
miles away at the other end
of a telephone line, with the toddler left screaming
in a shopping cart, with a fifteen-year-old
mother, choosing which cans,
with the child dancing the leading part,
with the hopeless bride in her staining lace

as she glides back over the scarlet path,
with the dog in the square and beneath the tree,
with Jack and Mama and the guys around town,
with the man on his back about to die,
with Crispin and Michael and all who are saints,
with the man in the loggia and the other's wife,
with the people in books and with gingerbread boys,
with the dreaming butcher wielding his knife,
with those who lift their hearts in a cup
while the wheel spins on and the slip drips down,
with the one voice claiming *I live a lie*
and with all who feel they live that way....

> Dear Riva, bright
> shadow,
> somewhere a door
> to slip silently through stands
> slightly ajar
> and spills a clean light. Lead me
> to that glowing kiln and
> balance me within. Riva, my heart
> throbs like that, cools like that fire.
> *Where are we?* Please hold me now
> through this spinning
> night and whisper your simple words.

IV

THIS WAR, THIS WAS

I cannot tell you that you are all I have wanted, ever.
Nobody must know, and now you are never alone.
There was a time you lifted my hips to your own
(burning birch, burning pine). You tattooed my heart
with the shape of a hawk flying west in the sky, your tongue
rowing its wet song thighward, higher. Something loosened
inside me: unbraiding water, bread ... dismantled and scattered
for talons, beaks. What permanence there is for me, floats—bright
wrapper—on a slow-moving surface, while under crimped waves,
always, a tugging. In my sonnet called Bird Songs, I wrote:
"Now you are sleeping in someone other's arms." Thin bridge
spanning the wide plain between far-set eyes. Rain for two
days straight. A boat swallowed in fog. Each body of water
straining toward every other. This is not new news I'm reporting.

When you catch your fingers in the hair above her ear,
do you think of me (bergamot, creosote) ever? Steam fills
the clanking pipes with a promise of warmth. Elsewhere, sirens
and shells. Often: something fractured, shattered beyond identity,
but tenable as splendor of mica, abalone, mother-of-pearl. ... Scarves
of celery algae snagged on black rocks. Somewhere a telephone rings,
rings. Shards of zinc light, liquid jewels, slicking the tidal pools
with a late-night hope. And seasons: Clump of Christmas tinsel
caught in a shaggy fork. ... Shine in the spine of something stainless
halting me mid-syllable. ... Key in my hand raised in an attitude
of perpetual motion *toward*. ... Little bird, for you (tinder, tinder)
my bones burn. There is no song I can write for you now.
But know that since you have gone ... still, you are being heard.

SESTINA ABOUT RECIPROCITY

Two dimes and a nickel don't always equal a quarter.
We pay each other in foreign currencies. At the end
of another day, feet propped on a brocade ottoman,
we await your intended arrival. Your style
is to be late. We've decided you have your own sense of time
which we've learned is not ours. The smudged red
ball of sun begins to sink into elbows, knees, outflung arms
of pines. Nature knows a comfort
only one in love with herself can know. Confident
to touch everything all at once with no criminal
intent, to caress each one of us with abandon, to leave
us without word each day in a silken

darkness smattered by cold stars which wink
like eyes of slick, mean boys wearing raw silk
jackets, boys you know you shouldn't go with, but follow
anyway, knowing full well that in the end
they'll have you in a Saab or some compromising bed
of a red pickup, undressed. Which is the crime?
After all, each one asks us to go along. You never
told us honesty and virtue exist in the stylish
package you present to the world. Your personality
is three-quarters facade. We take comfort
in telling you such things, though we wonder whether
they ever reach your heart. Each morning, red

eyes give you away for having been awake all
night, or weeping. *I was reading,*
you tell us over breakfast, though we question whose
open book, whose hands and tea leaves, whose silk
sheets you spent the evening sweeping your eyes and
limbs across. You've worked out some comfortable
arrangement. Are you happy? We wait in our chairs
until quarter to twelve and in the end
we take ourselves to bed. We are miffed but secretly
we feel relief. We rationalize. Yours is a stylized
beauty which isn't true enough; you are no good for us.
Already, we have lovers, wives. Our eyes incriminate

us, though. Indeed, we do desire you. To rationalize
is to commit the most unforgivable crime;
hence, our decision to live on the edge, to ride each guardrail
through stormy nights, to let two tires of our red
Corvette kiss the air as we bomb through backwoods, careen
around hairpin turns, our headbeams two stilettos
piercing the dark fog fabric. Hundreds of feet off the ground
we must be willing to trust the ability of silkworms
to make threads strong enough to hold us when we leap
from planes. Our reservations are endless.

It helps to be pushed, and when you want, you push us.
        We ply you with shots of Southern Comfort,

we give you clove cigarettes to smoke and sweet morsels
        to nibble. We tuck our down-filled comforters
around your small shoulders, fearing that you might fly away
        from us at any moment. We feel driven toward *crime*
passionel, but could we actually kill you to keep you here?
        Two nickels for a dime, five pennies a nickel, an endless
number of ways to make change occur. In our transactions
        with you, each seductive gesture seems a potential red
herring hiding a more lucrative arrangement. For whom? Life's
        pleasures are temporary and not entirely for us. The silken
flattery you offer eases our fears momentarily, though
        often we debate virtue of substance versus style

in an attempt to convince ourselves that both are good. Many
        of us choose the single flamboyant stylist
if given a quarter of a chance. We give and take from her,
        relishing in private some degree of comfort
because she has others. Fortunately she doesn't want to give
        herself completely to us: we love her cornsilk
hair and skin, we love flirtation with its pretty possibilities,
        but to us, actual involvement is a petty crime
considering our responsibilities at home. Reciprocity is beautiful
        in the way it differs from equivalence. Red
means *stop* in a car on the line in Dubuque, but in Amsterdam
        red invites us to *come in, world without end,*

amen... Finally, reciprocity should have nothing to do
        with addition. We decide we can burn one end
of the beeswax candle, and still share its heat and flame.
        We will wait but irreverently; we will live stylishly
but with simplicity. If you come to us, we'll take from you
        your kind wishes and embraces, we'll kiss your red
lips. Certainly at times we must risk our lives to feel truly
        alive, but we mustn't always trade simple comforts
we have found already, for thrill. Reciprocity resembles honesty
        in that not giving is often giving more. The criminal
takes more than she deserves without giving back. The banker
        gives but takes note. The one we await, who is silk-

clad and late as usual, finally straddles us all like a turnstile,
        moves through tolls from city to country, sets crime
into the comfortable motion of a cantering palomino. We mean it
        when we say, *we were never more ready.*
A field falls at our feet, a silk handkerchief. We think it lies
        still, but in wind like this, the wheat undulates endlessly.

THE SPACE

Too late, when the wake takes shape I'm gone. Watch me move. Watch me moving.
Too late, when the wake takes shape I'm gone. Through. Feel me passing through you.

It was almost as if the thing her absence cleft in air remained suspended there even after
the room had been abandoned by all. Grackles caught in the flue, some insistent beam
piercing the keyhole, his far-off lantern swinging a smeary path from barn to fence,
the yawning silence into which she'd disappeared. Too late.

Oh, but look what's left.
What stays the same, by always changing.

*

By this I mean bodies which constantly alter in nature around a concrete shape. Always,
there are many edges rubbing together. Call it atmosphere, if it pleases you. But keep
in mind that when I say intrusion, my intention is hardly derogatory.

Picture, for example, the avocado: Reptilian hide, peeled away to reveal the light yellow
curds which cup in celadon the core, that wooden egg. I imagine you suspected I would
choose this particular vegetable. So much is quite predictable, it frightens us.

Rather than carving up the flesh, propping the seed with three straws across the rim of a
juice glass—go on, kneel on the floor, roll it away from you. If you squint,
its wake may take shape for you. Reverberations of air, lapping your face like waves.
The hiss which trails it, lovely coils of breath.

*

It was almost as if that which would appear invisible to any majority of people
had become the single most intrusive entity in her existence. Not, for example, that a cake
of almond soap has lost her interest. It is just that some expansion of air about it, as it slips
away, now concerns her most. Why, you ask? Well, I will attempt to elucidate her strange
behavior, since it is one we share.

More layers than merely shell and pith, for example. She's laminar as mica, and then
some. In fact, once you've reached her center, you realize how widespread the palpitations
from her single elements range in air. When she suffers a mere paroxysm, for example, a
sneeze or cough—the vortex spins around her, ad infinitum.

This is an approximation of an overlooked sensation occurring every other millisecond,
especially when objects remain stationary—that being the time when the weight of the space
grows heaviest. Accumulated heat, thick motes of mercurial dust.

*

In other words, don't go yet. Take another look. What runs the tunnel of your gaze and seizes there? You stain it. If you want something as substantial proof—go walk in the snow. It is not the bird but the sound which hangs in the air. Or bells, calling us to church. The cathedral without doors, can we enter?

*

Overlapping hours of argument. What functions as spiracle when the mood is dense as a fathom of sea? Once again, you are the child at the beach not wanting to be touched that way, behind the cabanas. Small aisles between the flaking boards, must-wet planks to run on. That didn't count at all. Seen from the side, what shaped the sky severely was his chin. The idea slips through the cicatrized mind like sand through a child's plastic sieve.

When you speak to me, I just want to touch you, even if only to gather the words briefly, in my upturned fingers.

If you lean toward me and I, away, it shifts but stays the same; this too if done in reverse. Altogether different, if we both come forward toward each other at once.

If it's a surprise, my lashes blink shut like an aperture, image caught on the inside of my lid. Consider, consider, then open. Oh, you wanted a kiss . . . Though,

sometimes if I move toward and you away, the space doesn't at all stay the same. Many cooler molecules thereby created make the space gape like a widening gutter.

How subtle. Her former lover sleeps with her downstairs neighbor one week later.

*

Lines of hay prepared for carting. Cleft in the sod, this seam of a barrel of bumped-up ground. What's sky sinks in between, more visible when there's rain—a perforation of a white-seeming nothingness, then, that which gushes from within. When you lie to me, I most feel the space I hide so wisely. *Genius loci.* I have a basic sense of time which you smudge out of focus, clearly. Tricky wicket, portalled inlet, leitmotif for all my life. Peeking through the eyelet edges, something fresh to wake the snakes. Such as, the smell of the sun.

Tonight, you might begin with paraffin, since it too seems without scent. Too late. Tonight, you might begin with one heart beating, since that is all we hear. Rather, what is only the fire, crackling hurly-burly in a sudden downdraft.

*

In the wake of all that, a lemma: the wedge formation of birds advancing in wind. The enviable capacity to span rugged acreage without falling in. Not to say that air currents pose no problems. But this capacious distance above, and the buffering zone of one in front! Why, a disposition such as this makes us each feel a bit vulnerable. Slumped down in the slick arms of the V, we're like a beetle, unable to climb up. And inverted— tropopause for a nomad! Oxygen thinning and all that. Like breathing water before they pulled you out. What a scolding you caught, but sympathy too. Who was that sculpted man slicing through the pool? We thought you were safely ensconced with that ancient sitter.

Isomorphous drifts of elements your skiff glides down unmanned. Each end a dam with cracks. And breathless freight, waiting for some sign. All hell in a handbasket, that is, and one which the chaff leaks out of. So laugh, if you must. Just don't jostle the eggs like that. Anyway,

at least, let's go somewhere. We've displaced air one too many times? Let this be most lasting. Thin spokes whirring us off, slicing the pie-shaped pieces of blue and pebble— while a kinetic carnival waits. Salmon rosettes pinned to the cart-wheel centers, don't even waver. And everything's tailed by a shipwrecked tunnel of dust.

*

Snipping greenery from a blue delphinium she slices her thumb. Consider, if she were to cut away her limbs how little she'd displace when soaking in the tub. Tiny wooden foot, tracing a scar across the battered fields. Caliber, hubbub. Dormer, skive. Her stream of blood thick in the sink, and all thoughts draining away with hollow suds.

When alive, she trips lightly as an aria. High-spirited, and often downright flighty. If that's a common denominator in our behavior. Yet, having abandoned flesh, does the mind spread further?

Either way, here's a clean slate. Take it. Too late?

Gestures eclipse all words. Scribble in air.

GRANTED

—for Juls

That which can't keep living, lives
in this love I have for what burns most
brightly, flaring even briefly, singing a song
so beautiful its shape is etched in air
long after its singer departs. As when at
summer's end in City Park I knew I was alone
again, though still I walked beside a man
for months my lover. Ten flecks of light
igniting the Ferris wheel's spokes
crawled crablike across the black
divide of sky, an elegant dressage of
phosphorescence, shifting through the oaks.
Knowing that what warms consumes & craving it.
Stepping close. But knowing when
to let go.
                          Heart-racing love
like the hummingbird, immaculate
& rare, dipping into lilies for nectar. All
slender, emerald & motor. Its wings a loud
smear, so quickly gone. What living takes
& gives. In a letter, a girl friend writes
how they tried repeatedly to kill
what finally killed him first—by aiming
minute laser beams as close to his heart as
possible. Then knowing they had to stop.
She loved him; he was twenty-six. That which
can't keep living, lives in this love
for what gives itself completely, holds back
nothing & thus briefly, holds us all
mouths open in rapt attention. A firework
explodes high over the crowd, a sound
deep enough to feel, then falls in silence.
The cascade of its dying
lights each face & there
                          keeps living. Once
years ago I stopped the car for oysters
at a makeshift place somewhere near Sauzelle.
Tired of being alone & hungry, I parked
by the shack which sprang from its
shell-strewn lot above dredged-out flats
where salt had once been gathered. Covered
myself with salt & blind from the glare
of sun off sea at the island's southern point
where I'd passed the day on horseback

pounding through the surf, I pushed
my way inside, stood waiting while
shapes emerged & finally composed a room
in the cool, dark air. By then grown
shy, made awkward by a man who
slipped his stiff blade into each sooty
split, scooped the pearl-grey nubs away
from their smooth pink beds & with an easy
grin handed me several barnacled, lace-edged
shells, I tipped them back in silence, juice
sluicing across my cheeks & was relieved
when the door slapped in:
                                        I wished
that I were one of *them*, her platinum hair
clipped in a cap, fit her fragile skull like light
& the way he gathered & bound, he seemed
a panther. Voices a warbling birdsong,
they plunged bronzed arms into each black
basin & finally chose the largest crab
I'd ever seen. A giant blue jewel
suddenly sprung to life: eight legs, two
pincers flailing through air. That which couldn't
keep living, an instant, a creature held up
against the cloudless sky in such a way that
momentarily all three blocked the falling
sun & became vast, linked silhouettes *still*
lives. Then, with green bottles of wine brought
from the cooler & stowed & the beast wrapped
in paper, they sped off in a tiny red roadster—
clinking & laughing, taking nothing or everything
for granted, erased in a wake of clay plumes.

FOR YOUR DEPARTURE

I am making an origami wagon for you.
I am folding the little yellow edges of this pad in
across the heart and sending it on its way, clasping its message.
I am brushing away a few tears, telling myself to save them for spring when
the radishes will need watering. I am saying go crazy don't stress take it
easy take chances; I am eating my words. And like anyone, I am thinking
about the space between one morning and winter and
the sea too, between a shadow and its bird, between the "oh"
and then any other letter. I am sipping a little Sebastiani
because that is what we always do,
and I am twirling in the head a little from the shoulders up
the way the wind does high between buildings in Manhattan.
I am tasting individual grapes and the salt
in the blood on my lips, and now I am seeing myself
rolling this creaking heart through the alleys on a gurney.
I am not making one single cut and I am not planning to;
I have been creasing sheet after
sheet of scented paper, trying to get just this right.
I am finally admitting something, as the trains crashing through here
shake my cups from the shelves, and the demented, monotonously syncopated
wail next door like an almost forgotten IV, suddenly feeds me
something recognizable and wise, something I'd like
to repeat for someone else, yet the words are already lost.
I am remembering a particular sweltering night in Middletown,
New Jersey, the stagnant air even the cicadas
had given up trying to breathe, and then
the feel that glass of cold water made, swallowed too quickly,
and a concurrent sinking feeling
that even though it had been terribly hot and terribly dull,
even though my brother would always be older,
that that day in my fifth year of existence on this planet was gone, completely
and would always be. And this evening
I am aching the way the sky must
moments after a star has shot through the black night.

SEA GLASS

The sea glass comes to
rest at last on sand, though
it sees itself more in bright fins

and scales, in smooth glinting
facets of what moves through
what moves, too, all around it.

It senses home of sorts. It has
no purchase on the slipping
silk of surf, and needs

none—nothing, cares little
for currency, though it has known
possession, wears its knowledge

of what containment means
in a remnant impression
of diamonds around a straight

neck, an *m* or *R*
embossed or indented like
a long-healed scar. It feels

a phantom pain, for, of course
it is only a fragment, a
shattered bit of what someone

once tipped back full in his
rough hand, placed his lips
safely and without thought

around to draw from, then
tossed from the truck to smash
below on jagged rocks.

It remembers travel, foreign
scents and importation, hears
the foghorn and feels a cousin

to passing porthole panes
in pleasure yachts, dazzling
across the sea's venetian blinds.

Bathed in briny carbonation
it fears nothing, becomes part
of the pavonine mosaic, a

paving for bare toes to pick
over slowly. Fingers may
find it, lift it to guard

in a dry pocket or, stash on a
cluttered dash with keys, stubs
and wrappers—where it will lie

at the world's mercy, for
who hasn't—looking into mystery,
another sea above it, filled too

with winking fragments, grains of
long dead rocks not yet extinguished
that somehow reassure it,
that somehow reassure us.

HARM'S WAY

As if there were just one.
A speeding train whose track you could step out of
despite your wrists tied down. As if you could shelve it high up,
out of reach beyond the sweep of harm's black wing. Scurry to the back
of the chased rat's hole. Avoid breech birth, roll the barbed wire
of spat words into one smooth coil, rewind a film of the car launched
from the road like a toy in a child's hand.
                              The road, harm's way—a little like love
in that there is no other. Fall into, discover. Something you bear
like a mother's never saying no; something you weather like storms. Find
the hurricane hole. Survive. Like a storm of tears which clears the eyes, spangles
the lashes, makes vivid the sight. Insight from harm. Always a part of charm
and harmony; *harmos*, a feeling, a quality that attracts delight and leaves you
a little bit wiser. Ready. Refreshed to rise to a challenge. That's harm's way
—not always bad. Something
                              you get up from, lick your fur, brush off your lapels
or hips. Chew a lip. A bit like fate, but one you can avoid or alter. Fate gets you—
a clock like the truck rushing oranges to Illinois. But harm's way is different:
a distraction like surf sucking in, out. Attraction, revulsion. A bit like a drug, an
addiction, an affliction you begin to baby like a limp; in changing your stride you bother
your back. New injury. Last lap or run down a snowy slope. *Just one more.* Harm,
standing by the bar. The debating chicken in highway gravel. Deep water. *Asking.*
Harm's way, kind of like pleasure in that it has a rub. The lover saying *harder, harder.*
Not always inevitable. Harm, a wave hitting you sideways. Or missing, like luck.
Now you see it, now . . . Like a rock
beneath the sea's surface. Not unlike hope. You have to drive despite statistics, or fly.
Buy the house beneath high tension lines. A certain property that is consistently
inconsistent. Like faith, in that you have to believe
in what you can't see. *This will only hurt a bit.* How music in movies tells you
Something lurks behind the door. Harm finds you
                              caught by your hair in the lift, one sleeve
snagged in the press. Harm's the price; it's hurt's revenge, related to
shame. Torture's cousin, pain's agent. *We have our ways,* laughs harm. The tiny heat
of a single flame which ignites the fire that burns the whole town down.
                              How in a world with no chance
of harm, the cool open expanse of a hand pressed to a lover's brow wouldn't reassure;
the meadow wouldn't hoist its buttercups and blades like victory flags. Harm gives
reason to the chanted word, the incantation. Harm puts a hand in a pocket
grasping for an amulet. Some talisman or trinket assumed to have magical powers.
A powder to drink. You wake looking over your shoulder, not walking beneath ladders,
saying *rabbit rabbit*, crossing before you dive, learning to aim right toward it, point and
squeeze, look it in the eye, smile when you say, *Come on, Buster, lay it on me,*
hit me with your best shot. That's harm's way—*make my day*—a bit ballsy, a bit
of bravado masking the fear. Bear-trap
                              beneath grass. Puma behind bars. Fending off.

In boatyard talk, the million-dollar yachts *about to kiss.* Undertow. A shadow. Harm's way is to fall like night, a silent poison, rain into snow. Early or later, one after another. And I do what I can to move through it. *As if* there were only one. As if in harm's face, I could offer a single lit tea light on the sill, a beacon to steer you away. Spray tonguing the slick rocks, a fierce rip tugging, and the blueness as it descends each afternoon, as it lengthens, as it blues then blacks, then quiets out all together.

THE PILL

Reason being, it often comes to this. So that
at least at last she may shake down her hair,
let it fall like a curtain of dark water across her face, and see herself
as much in the shadowed *there*
as in that which most often bounces off
each single strand in myriad shining ways, and finally swallow such
quiet knowledge, gracefully.

Bright-stream-through-the-purple-heather,
Bird-in-the-hand-worth-two, Merry-go-round-with-the-high-up-ring-
teased-by-flecks-of-liquid-gold-as-in-old-Mister-Doctor's-grin,

Pla-ce-bo.
Bolus, beadlette smooth and hard, small
enough to swallow. Nothing
is so simple. If I am
able, being reasonable, I shall please ...

*

It has something to do with the vertical language of rain, if I say to you
the pill is a country, or that every person you know
resembles you in more ways than there are
flecks of powder
in the tiny tablet in your hand. Doppelgängers,
all. No surefire way to attain the smallest possible particle
seems to exist,
so you keep on crushing it. The action
is palliative, but still
the pill's innermost core *is* impenetrable. Lie
down here in my mare's-nest for a short while—just one more time. How we could
believe the farthest-fetched notions
about the machine we had invented together ever
actually demonstrating perpetual motion in any manner.
Taking two of anything necessitates a bit of quick thinking
when a third party calls next morning. Tell yourself: *I will never
drink in excess again?* Better,
save yourself for the *creme de la creme*, then drink in.

Leave the pill out in another storm like that and the whole song
will be lost for translation.

*

For all practical purposes, call it a device. Like vision,
sometimes it makes you believe
that alleviation of pain is imminent. *X* and therefore *Y*.

Why not *always*, you ask. Well, consider, for example
the X on a gunner's sight. And therefore? Let me suggest
that side effects can be rain